INVINCIBLE HORIZON

*Aiming for the prospects beyond the
conceptual walls of our world*

S.K. BANINI

Order this book online at www.trafford.com
or email orders@trafford.com

Most Trafford titles are also available at major online book retailers.

© Copyright 2013 S.K. BANINI.
All rights reserved. No part of this publication may be reproduced, stored in a retrieval
system, or transmitted, in any form or by any means, electronic, mechanical, photocopying,
recording, or otherwise, without the written prior permission of the author.

Printed in the United States of America.

ISBN: 978-1-4669-9089-0 (sc)
ISBN: 978-1-4669-9088-3 (e)

Trafford rev. 06/14/2013

www.trafford.com

North America & international
toll-free: 1 888 232 4444 (USA & Canada)
phone: 250 383 6864 ♦ fax: 812 355 4082

Acknowledgement

Perhaps, it may sound quaintly enchanting to say that the contents of this book were as a result of invoking the creative gods of the mind. To yet again expose me to the metaphysical corridors of poetic tongues; wherefore, the colossal effect of all, especially the emotional/love and editorial support, writing/image contribution and the inspirations from my wife and kids, most importantly the breath of life from God that has blessed me with the mind of the art, would not have been properly appreciated. Hence, I am thankful to all: my family (my wife, kids and etc.) and to God, the originator of life and the talent who made this book a reality.

Contents

I am not A Poet

I just play with the words
Sometimes I conjure the emotions of the people and it hurts
I speak to the peculiar reasoning of all wisdom
My detractors call it an invasion into the norm of the free will kingdom
Dear you
Blame not the hand that writes
Not by the mind that thrive
But by the conspiracy of the wind of doctrines
Blown against the vulnerable thinking of life
That shields me not
To evade the infectious culture of our civilization
So then I write that I am not a poet

When I was born

Tis a special day for them
It depends on the aura of life between
It depends on the reality on the ground
It depends on whether a mistake,
Or a preplanned gift to the world
Yet, I know that it shall
Forever remain sacred in my struggle for existence
Though I remember not;
The love,
The adoration,
The admiration and
The Surprise,
Also the hate and the disappointment gaze at me by all
Who saw me come in design and in the perfect of perfection
As original as HIS image desire

Though I remember nothing of the pain
The cry and the joy of she whose love remained original
Even when I grow sour and bitter to swallow;
Yet she thus held me dear to her heart
Even as I grow to become that which you see
That which you read, that which they talk of
And that the beast I became
Yet the Angel, I become
The sweet,
The sour,
If I become a loss
Then shall she cursed the sacred day of the pain
But when I become a profit
Then shall she bless, the gift of a day
When I was born

I wish, I wished, I wish

I wish there was no sin
I wish truth only proceeded forth from within
I wish love alone rule our hearts
I wish hate was the good brother of love,
Together a sibling;
Of good old righteousness and sin
I wish riches and poverty were lovers who shall forever
Remain in the romance of lust
I wish it was always day
I wish it was always today
I wish today was never sour and,
If it is, perhaps sour will distinguish between the
Different sweetness there is to taste and experience
I wish we did not have to die
If otherwise,
Death should be the prize of good life we seek not to fear

I wish there was no war
And if it comes, war embodies
The name of games to stimulate and evoke happy emotions
While pain and reward become the object of focus
Thus, the star in our crown
I wish all the smiles so bright and inviting is as it seems to be
From the core of happiness
I wish the adventure of yester year
Yields not to today's older reality
I wish I do not love to yearn for all that we desire
Or wishes that I do not have to wish for
I wish I wished I wish
When wishes were not a thing of the imagination

Hahaha, it was a good bye

Was a sunny afternoon
At his corner
Doing what he loves best
The living chimney
"Banini" and with that smile as usual
"Chris", the reply of the economy soldier
Then I walked to a living corpse
Man, you have a lovely family
Oh yeah? Thanks
How is your daughter?
You know how it is,
Hard to tame in the prime of youth
Yeah, I know, the crazy lines right
Hahaha
And that is how you say goodbye?
Any way hahaha at you there,
In the land beyond the reach of the living
Goodbye buddy

Obituary

Indeed, at the dawn of the news
Though the remembrance of this ordeal
Though the river of sorrow floweth forth from within
Though the silent cries of sympathizers
Depict the aura of a cloudy sunny day
And when the pain of nothing laid its cold fingers to him that was
It was all like a dream
Yet, that smile,
In the midst of segregated words
I read through the lines with heavy heart,
Mine eyes so weary
Damn it Obituary,
You do no justice to the situation at hand
Words meant to justify
Makes no justice to the picture;
They smile like it never happened
Yet, it feels like a dream
Until I saw the tears
She cried her heart sour
Oh why,
Why so sudden,
May peace harbor your rest
For He who watcheth over thee; the author
Holdeth claim to thy soul.

The Great Fall

When the great tree of the branches of bureaucracy
For the birds of young democracy
Fail to stand the storms of revolutions
Then comes the great fall
An end to the branches of hegemony
Thus, it spreads forth an era of darkness
When the leaves of civilization descends to the effect of the season
Thus, the flowers that propagate the pulchritudinous values of soft power
Descend with a dance of death unto the roots of the great power
Leaving the beauty of its influence in the beaks of authoritarian birds,
It devours the life of an era
While the smiles of the sun kills the balance of unipolar
For a generation of trees are born to new birds
To a new shadow of polarity
A tree with roots in the voices of the mass
Weakening any seed of dictatorship
Oh great mother of trees
Thy branches of influence
Paves way to the birth of a new balance of power
In the calmness of your authority
The storm of change disrupts the cycle of the norm
And again the great fall
Of a tree; a system of hegemony

Stubborn Individualism

I know it all
The trend of the day
Speak not for I speaketh
I, it is I, never you, never them

Hope of the future
Down to destruction I send your hope
Beautiful scenery; scented breeze of life,
Freedom only through my eyes

I hate the backward progress of thy success
The resplendent I
The naught of your accomplishments
I applaud with a closed eye
The brother, the sister, the mother, the father to benefit
The struggle for peace; my peace
The foolish warrior
Fools intent; smiles to your hankering aspiration
The make of a stubborn individualism
The fabricated peace among greedy foes
Feigned love,
Stupidly received
Oh thou obtuse personality
Floating not amid the rapid flood; synthetic world

If Love is A Crime

If love is a crime
I want to be a criminal
The stupid lover
Then will I be the infatuated police
Wrought naught to the passion of thy action
The moral militia
I will sneak a peek to enforce marriage values
To the blue moans of courtship bed
Then will I be an erected judge
I will sentence the thrust of my office might on procreation night

If love is a crime
Then will I value the ecstasy of relationship
While I foreplay the exciting offense
I will scrutinize every inch of the open case;
Thus, strive to solve with evidence from my doggy sniff

If love is a crime
I will employ the jury of my fingers
To explore the figure of seduction for any evidence
The criminals white cells
I will divorce lust and romance,
At the chamber court of sex

Amid Birth and Death

As a child I walk down the perspective path
A boy, a girl, the winds of direction contort the straight dusty road
To the surprise of the bend you become a slave
The horizon of life;
Birth and death vanishes in the midst of reality
As an adult,
The winds of visions and missions reveal the hard revelations
Blown to flirts of struggle and success
Then through the torture of manhood
Per the strength of your fight
The road appears thick of thorns to prick each step
Thus, you hop and step and leap to the end of a long winding life
Awaits thy smiles and tears,
Lays the deep sea of nothing
Amid birth and death,
The long wining road of wrath

If You Are Not a Poet

If you are not a poet
You write as though a poet
Every new thought you write
The style
It presence the self;
Thus, it feels as though a child's first grip at the pen,
A child first writes at his identity,
The couples stolen embrace in the corner of darkness,
An ungodly penetration into the unchaste virginity,
A mother's joy of the noisy cry of her begat,
You feel as though you are a poet.

So Little She Talk Like an Adult

So little she talks like an adult
Like the mother
Not wanting to hear the tyranny,
Of her child's play of noise
Dedicated to worrisome ears of life
As she speaks she rejects to focus;
Okay Kwame "Bye bye"
As I laughed to the doorway
The rejection of my morning kisses
Before the hard labor
To the amazement of my wife
Many a times our daughter speaks like an adult

Enough

She holds the phone to her ears
Her father's,
Her mother's
And when she does, tis never on
Yet the unknown voice at the other end
Seems to understand the chit chat;
The world of infants,
Aliens' language of a boring child talks
Ha-ha-ha, one word forms a thousand
One word form the lengthy conversation
Enough, ha-ha-ha, poor listener

But Who Is the Parent

So then I hold my pen, my paper
A biographer of the infant tales
So then I write these thoughts of life
So then I write the deeds of a life time
Waiting to write, I walk the walks of a child
While I stroll behind her fumbling legs
Ready to capture the stunt worth the work
My child, my dream
But who is the parent
The voice that passed by
The funny daughter
The words of a drunken father
Soaked in the toxin of love

Corrosive Waters of Failure

Where ever they are I will crush them like an elephant
They will weep like political enemies to my weight
Like the tyrant seeking imperial justice
To obliterate their united defiance to my untimely success

In a cause secluded to the nobles of my panoramic onslaught
Will I annihilate the demons in the institutional daemons
Bolstered by the grudge of fate
Thus, amid the corrosive waters of failure
Will the personality of my reparation drown
In thy evanescent craving to my aspirations

When the protocol of vengeance have been exhausted to no avail
Brutal alternatives shall be under the command of my lousy incentives
I will smile to your bravery, your weakness to the dispensation of my
    ascendancy
Along the sidelines of accomplishment,
Freedom from the mortifying fingers of detractions

They Just Don't Understand

They just don't understand,
Why you speak the way you do
Why you're clad in culture so different
Why the wild provides you protein
Why you smile to the suffocating grips of poverty,
Hunger, war, cultural dilemma, imperialism, friendly insults
Why the good Old man beyond the cover of the clouds,
The inquisitive glare of the moon stealing a peak,
In the shadows of his dark companion; nights
The billion soldier match of stars advancing to conquer earth;
Why under the command of heat general; sun
Planted you in the west or the worse

They just don't understand
Your stand in glorifying the author
Your life in death
The race of gods
Your trust for nothing but for something
Your birth in love
Your death to resolve
Your cry for their tears for living
Your quest for life beyond the space of nothing,
But your fear for life in the realm of the living

The just don't understand
The scriptures of science
The language of believers
The walks of reality
The loudness of night when the voices of nothing consume your faith,
Whilst speaking in the tongues of dreams
The darkness of light; blinding with the waves of colors
The coldness of heat, when it strikes with the rod of pain scorching
    with values
The beauty of mysteries in the path of shadows
Whilst the horizon approach behind

Invincible Horizon

Invincible horizon
Thus, the victory strategies well laid
Yet, the symptoms of hope eludes further
Beyond the blinding beauty of success
Where the rewards of fate,
Awaits hopelessly to flirts off an unrewarding ambition

Invincible horizon
Pregnant with invincible dreams of life
Loyal to the winds of doctrines
Yet, drifted ashore by the waves culture and values
Oh thou grand master, stretch forth thy hand of inspirations
For I'm drowning in the generational ideas of oppressions
Whilst the boat of reasoning afloat the body of flesh
Hence, without the compass of judgment

Invincible horizon
As I walk bare to the skin
The thorny ground reminds of dreams unconquered
Yet, the destination of aspirations
Outwit the race of reality
Millions of years have I walk
Yet, my rewards seems beyond the stars
Along the banks of life
The beauty my words sets
Floats beyond the horizon

Invincible horizon
Visible to life, natured by longevity of propriety
Such is the walk of warriors
Weaken by the pain of hunger
Stiffen by the stress of agony
Outwit by the swiftness of your predator
You rest not for the nurture of failure
As you walk chest high
Amid the thick of stagnation,
The exit if success comes to your dilemma.

The Quiet Man

He dwells among the mountainous minds;
Living off the skills of quiet thoughts
Archaic; he's the outdated man,
As the fingers of the accursed civilization remits
They float through life as dead leaves descend carelessly to its fate
Dead to its identity, dead to their culture,
They call him primitive
Yet, tis the quite man; pre-empathy preventive

Out of style says the fingers of many
Born of yesterday
He lives among the blind generation of complex visions
His ambitions, led to life by the bravery;
The light of tomorrow
He is the seed of the lost values
Seeking the fertile mind of life
To cultivate the myth of the fathers
Tis the quiet man,
Principled, though the noise of culture, tradition

Peculiar zeal, the lone army to victory

Thus, they Fear the reproach of history

Whilst the religion of perception enslaves the envisioned children

The burden of culture battles the logic of reasoning

He is the quiet man

The wired ability of his age

Enslaved by the intelligence of the confused mind

Thus, the work of wisdom,

The window to the past and to the future

Fingers of Critics

If not my friend, when sprouting with life
My adversary ye shall remain when I bare them fruits
For you will not have any part in the harvest
Even when gloomy the labour of your liars' sweets mine ears
Even when I'm drowned in the quandary of woes
Even when lost in thy knockout bewitching personality
I will look and see you not
Once I bare that mark of unequally yoked
I will marginalize the conscious from the conscience
And when the fingers of critics stare my way
Hence, the agony of yesterday will hinder your sway
For your era was,
Now the rains of success floods mine hinterlands
Once a desert; paucity of the currency
Now soaked in the rains of the wet seasons
The rewards of a striving labour
Thus, I harvest with greed
Sway me not,
Ye covets eyes of friendly adversaries
For I will give no acquittances to the labour of critical fingers

Yaa Asantewaa

Born to be the mother of warriors
The commander of the colonized revolution
The emblem Power and sovereignty
The queen of beauty, the queen of the Wild West
As the beasts of oppression falls to her feet
Fortified by the aura of war
She seductively danced to the bravery calls war drums
The enchantment of the merchants' warriors
As she defies the valor's greed; the culture of men
Yet, she bowed not,
Not to the masculine slurs of passionate assassins
Not to the pressure of male pleasure
For she is the fortitude queen of the coast of riches
The mineral crusaders,
The invading ships of hegemony shall fall;
To the grips, to the greed, to the waiting hands of death

As she torcher with her nude;
A sagacious strategy, a weapon of male destruction
The African beauty
Deathly seducing
Queen of warriors
The terrains are indeed bumpy
Yet, they dare not strike with their crutch
For she kills with the strength of her bosom
Yet, she wails for the death of her adversaries
She respect the land of deceased
For she is a mother, a queen and a lover
The commander in chief of the colonized revolution
The Joan of Arc of Ghana
Yaa Asantewaa

Anokye

Anokye, the past sings to your disappearance
A contemporary proletariat of your kind
We revere your celestial deeds
Yet, the greed of today leaves no identity for the dwellers of tomorrow
Whilst the light of yesterday walks not our way no more
Now a culture of injustice;
For we bear the creed of the crusaders greed
Oh Anokye,
The hope of tradition,
The hope of culture,
The hope of our identity,
Where are thou; the son of the land
The begotten of our ancestors
Come thou priest of the spirits
To summon the stool of unity
For the kings of today seek for the sign from above

May your golden stool of culture descend to resolve
For the symbol of freedom and justice, we bid thee to invoke
Yes, invoke that spirit of unity
Amid the clouds of uncertainty,
The drums of war calls for the purifying blood of its warriors
We the soldiers of Africa,
Seeks to avenge the demise of that culture,
Seeks to reclaim the tradition of peace
Oh thou great Anokye
The priest of the sacred stool
Return from the phantom's journey
Return with the keys of life
Bring to us the victory you promised
For the republic awaits your return

Tis life

Now I feel that zeal
The feeling I had about two years ago
The feeling of which lacks definite language
Tis that zeal for life
Tis life
That which clouds over the melancholy of failure's dominion
Yet, tis a cloud of passion
That shakes off the foundations of stiffen realities
The dirty works of melancholic hiatus
Whence thou come brings to me joy unspeakable
The fortune town of favor where we all originated
Presents to me the smiles of life
Tis life
Of the Helens of mine loins

A ride with the boys

I sat relaxed in a belly of the big iron serpent
Whilst I become the nutrient to feed the economy
The daily bread for its covetous tradition
Yet, I enjoy the scenery of nature's ride
Presented in quick flash moments through the forest of it course
At the end of the cycle
I will be emptied to face the system; capital labor
But at the point when my importance has been exhausted
Likewise the digestive systems
Thus the revelation of the ride becomes
A beautiful thing of the past
A ride with the boys
Amid the serpent on wheels

Never Again

Never again will I begat from the shadows of expression
Never again will I endure your whips and back stabbing slur of your
    soft power
Never again will the secrets of my past generations, the earthly
    blessings of my shores
Be a thing of the past, disguised to be revisited

Never again will the mirror of deception entrap my innocence
With the fabricated power of self-destruction that ye fear to flirt with
Never again will the sweat of my blood fill the machinery of deathly
    power
Never again will you be drunk in the innocence of my youth and the
    strength of my life

Never again will the hate of the old moon brought by greed of
Her light be the memories of my agony
The point of my sorrows, the barrier to my progress
Nor the prize be malt water to my revenge about peace and love
Never again will I be preyed upon by the beauty of their brutal embrace
Never again will I fear my past my future

One Night Stand

With the grips of a Warriors love,
I firmly clench my hands around
It's contoured bottom,
And when it stare's;
Great was its beauty that it flirts,
Away the thought of ever betraying
Thus I thrust with the barrel,
Of my friend my weapon, hence my
Envisioned adversaries,
Obliterated at first thrust
Of a soldier's charge to victory
Glorified in my heavy breathings;
And at the peak of destruction
Amplified by the moans of a dying soldier,
I wiped down the red seed of life of the enemy,
That drains down the rigid and unyielding

Weapon that a soldier bare
Staring down the battle field
The lifeless figure of my victims lies
In a pool of life
Thus I smile at the handy work of my bravery
While the promise of achievements
Drain from my face down the skin
Yet, another medieval vision
In a decorated Infantry man
Deep in the glory of one night stand
Brandishing my sword in excitement
What a victory the night brings,
Tis a one night stand

In the stillness of this afternoon

In the heat of the day
The sun so bright
Yet, the clouds claim its share
Of nature's grudge with humanity
I step out from the captivity of my freedom
And I'm welcomed by the stillness of an active afternoon
Leaves on the trees enjoy a quiet time
Then it dawn on me
The reflection of homeland
Their brethren in the motherland
Keeping a busy schedule;
Charcoals for life, fire for a civilization
Oh African trees, I wish you could enjoy this
Peace that I hate to bare
When the winds torments not
In the stillness of this afternoon

Generation of war

The sound of war
The big booms of rockets, grenades,
Death from above
When the big metal bird drops the eggs of war
The ratatatatatata of heavy artilleries,
The cries of AK 47's and its siblings
The agony on the battlefield
Blood stained warriors of the greed
Scares me not
For I am of the generation of war
For I am a descendant of the soldier
I am stained with the blood of those who kill me
When they run from the reproach diplomatic crime
When they hide from the monsters of war
When they choose death to not heed to commanders of doom
When they feed on flesh to survive the fate of warriors
I press on because I am not afraid
I am the gene of that deathly system

A generation of killers

A generation of killers
The norm of the society
They thirst blood to seek unity
A profession of assassins killing with diplomacy
Snipers of civilization killing with education
Murderers with the vote of consensus
Who bully with one accord
Who run from the fear by creating fear
Oh what a bloody peace
When our fate lives in the straying bullets
And in the disease of doctrines
Oh what a fate
A generation of killers indeed

I love you, my wife

You are the best mom
You are the best wife
To be compared to just the best thing is so below par excellence
Because you are the throbbing peace of my existence
My heart
My life
My joy
My sheer existence, drives on thy love sweet heart
I will not forget the breath of life that you keep not to thy self only
But breathe into the product of our love
Even through breast feeding the little ones
And even through de delicious delicacies presented to my table
At the break of the day
And at the dead of the day
You strive for what I am

Yet I reward with the strife of pain,
While I speak with man's superior foolishness
And the exposed bravery of lonely warriors
Oh what a beast I am
Oh what a shame I am
Love, I shall forever remain enslave to thy love
Thus, I decree to my heart,
To obey, obey and obey
Because you are the youth in me
Growing each day with beautiful potentials
The newness in me that,
Screams to light up this darkness of a day
Never will I ever betray thy un-tainted love
Come to thy cage of affection, my beautiful dove
I love you, my wife.

My Mother

My mother
She bare the pain of nine months
She spared me the last for her mouth
Though her path to love swirls about like a labyrinth
Yet, she cares less for my roughness

My mother
When the trials of life hit me hard
When the cycle of success evades me to look so sad
Yet, at the sight of me she smiles to the skies, for the joy of a child
    made her glad

My mother
Though the promise of tomorrow may shine to naught
Though the strife she thrived may reward not
Though the grounds she wished me to gain may seems to trot
Thus, in the pit of frustration she lifts her child not to rot

My mother
Though her age may frail, yet, her love for me remain the same
Though my wrongs may pile up to the lips of foes, yet, she stays to
　　care without a pin of shame
And when the fingers of hate will seek to stain me in the lies of greed,
　　she stands a wall and finds me no blame

My mother
I love you,
Many a times have I dared your wrath
Yet, in cheers have you loved me to live
Though I fell several times in the path to maturity
Yet, you stood to fend off the pain of nature

Share no Tears

Little girl, little girl, share no tears
For daddy will come and take away your fears
Dance to the clap for your mother is here
Sing along with me, let the whole world hear

Little girl, little girl, share no tears
Embrace the Lord; He will be your friend
Do away with shame and let's just blend
No more fights with your siblings, but amend

Little girl, little girl, share no tears
Let not thy crave be the cause of your pain
Listen to your mother and your father to your gain
Don't be like them when they do things in vain

Little girl, little girl share no tears
Listen to advice; you reap what you sow
When you do as you are told, your heart will glow
Let the joy of love drive you to grow

Poem

Poem is good
Poem is life
Tis the secret code
Amid the heart,
The soul and the flesh
Tis driven by passion
Thus, deduced with a vision
Tis a fallacy; myth to the extraneous mind
Yet, to the preordained; a gift untouched by civilization to mankind
Read the reader's lips and the words exit with style
Whilst the countenance of the confused, amazed the poem to smile

War Child

He is the byproduct of resolvable hostilities
An emblem of a generation with stolen identities
A tool to feed the cravings of an era of greed
The victim of war culture yet a perpetrator of an imposed creed

She will be the mother of blinded little warrior
A generation of brighter horizon
Her back lies to the crutch of lost aggression
The bread of life, yet sadly inferior
To the filth of brat soldiers of home grown imperialism

A progressive culture of stressed societies
Drunk in the blurry lies of the embattled world
The war child, reject by the ideals of imperial democracy
Imposing the rule by the force of law
Thus, the shadow of anarchy cast upon the mornings of a sunny day

A Dream of Class

Tis that dream that we so yearn for that impedes the dream

Tis that which we seek to liberate us from the clenches of nothing

A dream that rebels against the tyranny of enslaved potentials

Tis the appraised ambitions

The potent transfiguration of visions

The machinery strength of them that seeks the class beyond the dream

Tis that dream which ought to save

Yet the dream that kills the dreamer

Tis the seducing revelations

That ceases not to invade the privacy of our ambitions

Tis that dream that I fear not to dream

Yet tis the dream that rules the world of class

Tis that which many strive for beyond the horizon of their homeland

Tis the generation of dreamers where the addicted dreamer regrets not

Tis that dream I dream to walk away from; the dream of class

Drawing

Beautiful delicacy, I draw you in the rich words of desire
In my thoughts I sketch you in the nude
I feel the passion of yester year's artist
When the only camera is the stroke of my brush
The chance to see beauties they draw to touch
Tis the faces of the maidens, smiling lust to my strokes
The smiles illuminated by sweet spread of the lips
As I shade off the stealing glance of the nosy lights
Your windows of life revealing the affections to drawing rituals
Quick peak reveals a still framed goddess of love.
Oh what a master piece
Your pose speaks silently to my heart
Perhaps, I may lay down my tools to come spend eternity with you
Yet, I am at the mercy of my strokes to keep you alive
Lest I rob you off the beauty that steals my sight
Then to the sight that man lust to see
The bosom of blossom maiden
The place of bond between a mother and a child
Yet a bond of lust with passion in times the sacred union

This is love

This is love
At the dawn of breath
Drowned in amniotic fluids of warmth
Entangled by the cord of shared life
She reaches for her likeness and embraced to care

This is love
Stiffened with the cycle of family survival
strangled by the paucity of labor mercies
Abused by the imperative of thy quotidian bread
He smile with ease at the peace of his happy family

This is love
When the fantasy of desire is transcended by age and reality
When the cloaked emotion is anticipated as flirts
When the first sight soaked you in blush of affection
And when the leap of faith bust out of the cage of flirts
To conjure out the unyielding love of lovers to be
Crowned in your ring

This is love
When death does come
You share a tear naught of pain
You share a tear naught of hate
But for the memories of good old deeds
And seek not of human greed to retain the sick of their pain

Life in Death

Life in death
A civilization of a religious culture
Promised to the faithful; the mysteries
Amid the realm of celestial beings
A seed of one true tree
Yet predators to their ingrown doctrines
Feeding on the skills of assumptions
Whilst the true fruits remain caged in doctrinal shells
Hidden from them that seek not
Thus revealed to the seed of the first begat
Who seek to crack open the shell of deception
And devour the fruit of life
To die to this civilization of death
And to a birth of revelations
Life in death

State of Anarchy

A bandit of rights
Exorcised but to the civilization of doom
Chronicled by terminal voices of all
Unfortunate symbol of anarchy
Thus, a generation of suicidal liberties
Perpetuated by political omniscience
Whilst being captives to democratic hegemony
A state of anarchy
Revered as the rule of law

The Sacred Wardrobe

The evidence of my existence
Amid the chaos of space
Hence the accumulation of attire
To cover up the original
Yet, to cover up the desire of that revelation
Tis the sacred wardrobe
Home to generational divide
Within the corridors of human rest life
Where species of garments lay in the comfy of human absence
The beauty of culture displayed to mine contemporary ideals
Batiks, the custom of Sub-Sahara to style up ready-made west
To grace the walls of a sacred wardrobe

Face of Pain

Amid the clutched hand, lays
The legacy of murderous rituals
Yet, the legacy of modern generation
Heads bowed to the shame
He alone dwells in the state of nature
The tears are dried
The bodiless head reveal a face of pain
Resting in bloody fate
The gruesome hands of authority
The soldiers of anarchy
Tossed about in the furry of authority
In the sea of yearning guns
He awaits his fate
Yet, the generation life presides
Can death prevail or pain defend
Whilst the order of today dwells in the wild of nature

A feast for the uncivilized creatures
The ghost will tell
The bone will reveal
Thus sayeth the face of pain
Speaking to mine emotion
Speaking to mine anger
Speaking of that state
When I wish to wrought to him nature fury
No longer can I bear
The cry for help
The tear that floweth not
The eyes that opens, yet sees not
The countenance of agony
Thus, the face of pain

The Mirror of Life

Seated in the shadows of her abode

She stares astonishingly at the nude figure that smile back at her

For once the reality of the moment evades her

As she spun to steal a peak at whom the mirror smiles

Revealing the bare bosom of an aging life

A beauty beyond the myth of Helen's

Yet a mother of many refined maidens and warriors in her likeness

Today she stares with curiosity at the strange lady in the mirror

As if smiling away life

But the folds of age, along the once bumpy terrains of her nude
    reveals otherwise

Amid the comfy of loneliness

Before the reflection of boredom

Away from the intricate of reality

Away from the prying eyes of garments

The mirror of life tells no lie

I Thought I Saw Me

I thought I saw me twenty-nine years ago
Intrigued by the sight of history, I admire yet I feared
It was said they had come from the skies;
From the unknown creator of the universe
Falling as gods in the tales of our elders to battle my people
It was said, they descended from the vessel of power
It was said that they came from beyond the reach of the seas
There, where the fate of our future heads
Away they go to the shores of no return
To the shores of the fallen gods
To the mysteries of western tales
Thus, I stare
Yearning to touch, as the smile of curiosity of mine youth eludes fear
But the tales from beyond the seas of oppression
Reprimands mine youthful ambition
Kwame, the young they take to the shores of servitude,
Return not to tell of the greed of the explores
Now courage builds to transcend the fear
Thus, the slang OBRONI escaped me as the alien tongue "Irish,
    Irish" runs me away
I ran, carried away by the bare foot of youth
Amid the dust of today, the clouds of a new generation
Screaming "Irish, Irish" to my amazement
And to the exit of my dreams

The Gift from Above

From the age of the mornings to the age of the evenings
We are still explorers to the lands beyond the horizon of life
We remain sucklings to the watchful eyes from above
Life rejected as we flirt with the alluring horror of death
The child's play that kills
Toys of iron, toys of death
Gift of power to the bullies of infant generation
At the playground of war, the element of life
Conjured by curiosity to halt the breath of life
We look to the skies for new grounds to play on
To the skies for the gift from above
Yet, to the skies for death from above
Thus, at the mercy of hegemonic birds of war
To the plight of the weak
To the promise of the faithful
A gift or death
We look to the skies

1957

Born to be great
Impediment to the greed of imperialism
The shining star of a dark civilization
The rigid lies of big brother of the vessels
Drummed to the tongue of the natives
Thus, they marched to the walled city by the coast
To volte-face an imposed destiny in 1957

Beneath your staggering grounds lays the beautiful wealth of evil
Yet, the gong-gong man, the voice of authority
Speaks to the ignorance of today; forget not thy future
When forced to the shores of oppression
The weeds of the forests now out grows our societies
Yet, the spirit of a dying generation labors in vain across the bridgeless
    river
Again the gong-gong calls to the forgotten woes of our fathers and
    our mothers
Break the chains of greed
Tear down the cloak of fear
Together we wave the blood banner of 1957

Come to the courtyard of warriors

Dance to the drums that bid thee to arms patriots,

Hide thy fears oh ye martyrs of today, let the bosom of thy wives and
mothers comfort your woes

Breathe your last to the guns oh ye faithfuls, justify your cause

See to it that the generations after leaves the shores of the motherland
in chains no more

May the future sing to the history of 1957

That we lived, we died, the blood freed our culture

My Country

It lies beyond the sea of sand
Unburden by the plundering roots of life
Graced across the ocean, down the forgotten west
Un-fished off of its values by the adulterated traditions of the sailors
Cruel to the wild, yet at the mercy of the cause of nature
It journeys the course of the survival,
My country

Protected by the might of two oceans
Tis the envy of malevolent aggressors
Held hostage by the cultures of nations
Oppressed by the fallacy of seducing rights
The protector of the capital world
Anchored in the power of the mass
Carved out of the fist of imperialism,
My country

Reclaimed its inheritance
Battled the power of the kings
It bares the spirit of an ancient empire
Tis perceived; the imperial republic
Armed by the strength of digital economy
From the west to the west
The old and the new,
My country

Condemned Carriers

They, Susceptible to the invading viruses of wild ambitions
The perpetrators of the cessation to the cycle of life
Yet, the condemned carriers of death amid the generations of rights
A horrible fate of the idiosyncratic progeny of civilization
The incorrigible fingers of permeated culture
Why blame the laws of life
To justify the venom of greed
Oh leaders of my people
Why do you whet the appetite
When the amorous engagement to suitors from afar
Yields a step forward to path the way for the two steps backwards
Hear the lamenting voices of the spirits yesterday
It echoes the woes of the aboriginal race

Why War

Why war
Why not peace
Yet, I warn; woof, woof, woof
Though I bark to the cause of peace
They throw bones at my feet; who said I am hungry
They care less for my life, I am only a pet
Yet, I sniffle out their dogmas of death in the game of pain
Woof, woof, woof; I am born to strife in the wild
Yet, they domesticate my potentials with their ambitions
A guard at night when they lay in the comfy of their bed
Yet, a friend in the morning fed with bones
Woof, woof, woof; Creatures of destruction
The beast of four or the beast of two
Who has the brain
I am a delicacy to the greed of civil hunger
Yet I love to bark them out of death
Woof, woof, woof
Why war
If only they will hear me, tis I, the pet barking again; Woof

Winter Comes

So bright my birth complements hope
Snowy youth, you shed light over gloomy summer of aging
Enough to the seasons of heat
Enough to the mysteries of hope
When maturity serves the labor of life
Yet, winter comes with the chills of potentials
To liberate you from the clutches of aging ambitions
And when the cycle of life reincarnates your potentials
Winter comes not only with youth
But with the exhilarating wealth of hope
The promises of birth, the promises of youth

Morning Gospeler

Generation of fabricated smiles
The sweet and sour ideals of the run-away civilization
Tarry not to the cleansing land of retribution
For the evening's wrath comes,
The morning gospeler
Now you sing to the farewell hymns of the nights
Will you not ride the redemption chariot?
And escape the cloaked path of the wailing failures
Invade not the trust of the sunlight while you sing sweet to the ears
Oh you master of pretends
Though thy lips whispers to the ears; the melody of the morning
You remain the lord of the night
A cloudy soul that scorch like the sun
Yet, I rest assure,
For the stars may not reveal the face behind the mask yet
The moon thus shines to the naught of your gospel

Killing Death

Why kill them who are dead?
For they live as though dead
Yes, the blood of the innocent stains the robe of culture
Yes, the blood of aggression nourishes the sword of justice
Thus, a civilization of death,
The battle ground for culture and politicks,
Whilst the umbilical cord of nationalism
Severed by the brute of religion and internationalist's wars
The justice we seek is to kill death
For them that we send to the gallows
Goes to the land of peace,
To their wishes with expectation; resting in peace
Thus, the reward to their deeds; a sanctuary to their evil,
Yet, you grant with the justice of modern law

He Planned It

Nothing seems to have been planned;
A candidate for the water closet baby,
Even worse, a child of the trash bag culture,
Perhaps the generation of lust relations,
Confined in the lonely soul of the orphan!

The child of many parents;
I roam in the confidence of tribulation virtues,
The child of a mother,
A reward to the greed,
Self-centered masters to naught,
The mark of today!

A child to failure,
A child to poverty,
A child to a dream,
The "It" of the ignorant projects,
The property of generational divide!

Molded from the thought of the great ONE;
I am the seed of the great old tree,
I am a fruit of life,
Protected by the branches of the tree,
Amid the garden of life;
Untouched by the pressures of life sucking insects,
Untouched by the civilization of death,
I am hope to that child;
HE planned it

Dance with Me

I sing the words,
Meaningless, as it tune to thine ears,
Unprecedented, as reasoning steal past your hearing,
Thus, it relaxes the yearning soul off the dancer,
Drunk to the complex images luring your thoughts,
I come to your mind, like the honeymoon night,
Evading the barriers of chastity in the quietness of your curiosity,
Dance with me, of these wars of words;
Yet, the melody of wisdom,
Rhythm to mine mental overtures,
Like the steam of thoughts;
Streaming out of its captors,
The brain of the poet

We are all generals

We go to war, motivated by the spirit of their ambitions,
Yet, how we live
How we die
Are the deeds of the warriors in our hearts,
Thus we are all generals

Where to aim,
Who to pull that trigger at,
Whether a smile to the good tears of victory
Or a cry to the pain of vengeance,
Tis the cause of a soldier's dilemma;
We are all generals

And when the aim goes astray,
And when the dead are only victims,
And when I am a sniper of fury,
But not ammunition for justice;
I stand alone, dressed for a trial thus, a prisoner of war amongst my own
Yet, I accept the verdict
We are all generals

Though a flag may be wrapped around the bed of rest,
Perhaps the sound of guns may be the fare well salute,
Though the stars for bravery he wears not,
Though the sacrifice ends not the struggle,
Yet, we go to fight;
We are all generals

Accra Academy

Bleoo, what a peace of a name,
Bleoo, an alias of a legendary school;
Amid the anarchy of day to day life of Accra,
It breeds the brains of intellects;
The machinery of a great civilization

Once a home to the consuming fortitude of a poet,
Untamed by the guise of knowledge acquisition;
We explored every facet of the academy par-excellence

Abound by the shared goals of the students,
We strive against the repelling forces of individualism,
Amid that city on the hill

O great Academy,
Your beauty imprinted among the greens of the ancestral trees of the land,
Yet, the tower of fate abides not only insight;
But by growling lion of knowledge and strength inside the academician
"The school of no regret"
Tis done Bleoo, bleoo, o great Academy

Point of Correction

Point of correction;
Tis the dawn of the living,
Amid the disparities of race and culture,
The beat of life is powered by the flow of red within the diaspora of
    humanity,
You are no uglier than I, the beacon of the unenlightened generation!

Point of correction;
Courtship with the living of the wild,
A taboo amid the first begat of humanity,
Tis I that call you to the morals of the great I am,
The era of doom, finding solace of lust among genders of a kind,
Let the furry fingers of thou cloaked beast lay to your iniquities

Point of correction;
Tis I, the product of hate
A merchandise of the greedy commerce,
The pivotal commodity to a lousy generation,
The rich effort of the poor class of race,
That replenishes, thus, feeds your hegemon avidity of power,
Thus, I beg not to differ, for I am no less human
Colonized values,
Leave me to wrestle with the collegial norms of a degraded generation

Africa

Rich and raw of origins
The striving power of thriving greens and the elements
Yet, the fabricated lab of all despised theories

Inhabited by the race of all
Exploited by the likes of few
Yet, the battle ground for the imperial siblings

Engaged to the greed of ancestral norms
Replenished by the dawn of new generation
Whilst upheld by the values of ghostly elders
Yet, a breeding ground for the beasts of greed

Though the laments of patriots, lingers in the clouds of today
They flirt with the invaders rosary of sci-fi success
O thou civilization of yesterday
Ruled by the vigilant fist of myths
Yet, tis the dawn of life
The origin of hope
Thus, I salute you Africa

When driven by the People

When driven by the people
It serves the cause of the living
It despises the depravities of colonial disposition
It yields to the norms of unity
And prevails against the tyranny of individual aspiration

When driven by the people
The gun smokes to the phantom of the liberators
It is not a passion of a profession
It is a demonstration off a revelation
Yet, it is the anarchy of the mass to invalidate the hierarchy of ring of
    class

When driven by the people
There is no lust for
Super-culture,
Exceptional influence,
Authority thus evolve into communal rights
While the national-cake, devoured by the creed of the rebellion
The distrust of mythical idealities, is engulfed by the flame of
    national unity

I Can Hardly Catch My Breath

I can hardly catch my breath
As it leaps ahead, to the sight of love
Unconsciously flirting out the burden of lust off of me

I can hardly catch my breath
As it skips the norm of the rhythm
While the eyes of the bachelor
Daydreaming to the beauty of your picture

I can hardly catch my breath
As it races to say yes I do
For the period of courtship seems to me like eternity

I can hardly catch my breath
As the dance of procreation overwhelms the sensual limitation
Thus, I yearn to be thy warrior, the night defender of your chambers

I can hardly catch my breath
As the strength of mine youth, capitulate to the weakness of aging
Yet, the passion of love burns like a teenager

I can hardly catch my breath
As the peace of mortality drain the life out of every breath I take
Yet, the voice of love calms me off the reality beyond the horizon of life.

To My Children

To my children
Live without fear of the toothless horror of today
Yet, live with the fear of Him that was, that is, and that is to come
For he is the reason you live
The myth of His suffrage is to your existence
Tis He, who will light your path, in the age of darkness
Tis He that speaks to your heart, your conscious self when you dare
    the wicked ways
He will not fail when I probed you not
He will love you even when you hate
He is the father of your father
And to Him we shall go when the hour is due
And life finds you worthy not to abide
Tis Him that creates and Him that destroys
Him, the living myth of my fathers
A fiction to the eyes of the blind
Life to the faithful

I Remember

I remember when I was a child
The dreams were wild
The mortal; feelings of living till the age begs me to naught
The invincible; I see not of the impediments of success
For the journey ahead was a horizon away
A child's dream

I remember the history of this future
The lust of this love
The desire of this devotion
The boy of this man
When he suffered the dilemma of the runner-up generation

I remember the rewards of those wrongs
The focus of my teens
The culture of lads in the prime of life
The dreams of boys to men
In the prime of age, when the errs of life; are the only adventure

From the Heavens

And when the storm of life floods my fate with desperations
And when the nut of love, wrenched out with the twist of infatuation
And when the course of life is marked by the prize of retrogression
Yet, from the heavens come the inspiration

Though the norm of tradition thus negate the cause
Though the creed of politics flaws my path
Though I bare the mark of pain, yet, I yield not to force
Thus, from the heavens decendeth the promised wrath

I have become the sole descendent of this identity
The natural rhythm of self-evaluation
I am the subject of a matter amid the forbidden integrity
But from the heavens I look to for the revelation

Human Rites

It is good that is why we like it

Very tender, smooth, an enticing culture to its core

Dreadful as the mass comforter

Yet, it has raging capabilities to its sweetness

Contrary to its power to life,

Tis the bait of the greed to an explosive fallacy of the conscious desire

But it is an idea

It differs in the mind amid genders

It is the human rites

I am a Soldier

I am a soldier
In the battles of the mind
In the battles of the heart
I conquer ideas

I am a soldier
A warrior in the political fallacy of a generation
An unapproved footman in an idiosyncratic warfare of the 21st people
Thus, the fatalist conqueror of your deathly ideals

I am a soldier
I fight to the voices of the people's cause
Yet, I retreat to the values of the mass
Thus, to revive the brutality of a good course

I am a soldier
The defender of novice virginity
In the politics of modern imperialism
I champion the sanctity of their chastity
I will penetrate every barrier of creed,
Thus, I dance to the appellations of victory morale

I am a soldier
The custodian of the captive culture
A martyr in the myths of the oppressed
Yet, I become a cancer,
The raging fire in the camp of the invaders

I am a soldier
Though a prisoner to foreign ideals, amid the camp of rivals
Though dedicated to the truce of economic gains
I remain a fighter, the first begotten of our cause

My Precious Jewel

My precious jewel
Can I adorn my dark deeds with your beauty
Can I wear you to the joy of my temperament
Will you be by my side as I smile to the reflection in the mirror
Will thy seed be mine as we romance to fate
Let the fate of life tarry as the joy of our union last

My precious jewel
I worship thy substance, but to thy creator my sole belongs
Bound by the order of love
Accept the pleasantries of covet eyes
As you lay, a showpiece of wealth

My precious jewel
You stir the heart of the living to yearn this wretched self
The riches of life have I not, but the wealth of love I give to thee
Hence, the pillar of influence you have bestowed upon me
From thy love, I am reminded of the endless strength of the corridor
    of hope
Thus, for these I will leave you not to chance naught

I Love it but I hate it

I love it, but I hate it
When the dilemma of the chorus runs
Freedom
Liberation
Salvation
Oh descendent of that kingdom
Let the light of that revelation illuminate the path to thy predisposition
Oh dissident of that republic
Let not the fallacy of sweet tongues derail the roots of yesterday's ideals
For the amnesia of this civilization seeks to converge the credence of
     diverging empires

I love it, but I hate it
When the slogan of politics seduce with
The honest facts of fabrications
The logic of professional liars
Thus, the intimidation by the weak
The few powerful
The generals imperial

I love it, but I hate it
When they are stained with the blood of their dreams
When the strength of their hope is rooted in the invaders cause
When they fail by their creed
Hence, the result of the past of the future, they blame to their greed

Sankofa

A generation of illicit concupiscent members
Return to the broken cistern of thy laws
Rebuild the walls of your morale's
Thus, wave to the culture of today, the values of the neglected morals
Yield not to the imperial storms, blown from across the seas from the
    east and the west
Sankofa; reclaim the dreams
Let the spirit of the past smile to the dance of freedom
To the cry of liberation
From the eternal dwellings of life
Let the cause of the ancestors prevail

Dilemma

I'm tired of you
I'm tired of this
I'm tired of it
I don't know if I'm tired at all

You; the trouble of life
This; obstacles invading my life
It; the unknown trespasses of my aspiration

Yet, I don't know if I should let you go
I don't know if this will hurt at all
I don't know if it even matters
Envy me not, ye eyes of covetousness
For I lay in the dilemma of the generous wicked cycle of life
Thus, I know not the pressure of good life
I prefer the pain of justice

Winding Road

The winding road of life

You are a spectacle of beautiful failures

Yet, your glory bestowed upon me, like the sourness of a beautiful wife

I walked through the ages of life

Slaying all the noble impediments of all stages

Thus, I docked at the bay of maturity

I dare you to come, O life's imperfections

For I yield not to your winding course of longevity

Come to me children of love

Descend unto my heart you puzzling romance of a dove

For I desire to bare the pain of affection

Now a master of yesterday and a novice of tomorrow

Come to me life

Come to me love

For I have conquered the uncertainties of today

My Mind

It is the mind of human
It is the thinking faculty of the conscious self
It is a being unseen that dwells in my head
My mind is I, the narrator of life

Though the eyes sees
It defines
The beautiful
The ugly
Though the nose smells it defines
The pheromone of lust
The aura of attractions
Though the ears hear
The voice of desire
The voice of rejection
It defines
What The lips may kiss, but my mind taste love

I am no different from that murderer
I may look just like that thief
Sometimes I grunt angrily like that bully
Yet, my mind sets,
The barrier
The limit
The differences
My mind regulates to the right

Rebellious Democracy

It is championed by the brutality of machines
AK 47
M 16
R.P.G.'s
Industrial and homemade bombs
Its cause is rooted in the philosophical course of anarchy
Martyrdom
Terrorism
Mass rebellion
It is the battle ground for the super worlds
The litmus test for the scientific democracy
The civilized revolution of a free world
Free off pity
Free off consensus
The politics of death
Amid a blind generation
Oh what a civilization

God never ordained them

The killing legacy of authority
Perpetuated by the positive aspirations of negative individualism
Thus, the norm of the minority; the dictator's brutality
God never ordained them

Imperialism
Colonialism
Exceptionalism
Emancipated wars amid democratic oppressions
God never ordained them

Leaders of provocational consensus of the new civilization
They enslave the dispositional values from beyond the clouds
While the vernacular of their motivation mortifies the yoke of their
    aspirations
God never ordained them

O monarchs of the industrial empires
Your gift of delusional liberties amid the democratic powers of the
    oppressed;
Executioners of tomorrow
The blood of your blood perish for your cause
God never ordained them

Politics to the unrealized dreams
Politics to the Book of life
Politics to the Father's vision
Politics to the plight of the weak
Politics to the success of your effort
Politics to the wisdom of intelligence
God never ordained them

True Love

It evades the strings of sex
True love nullifies pretext
It revolves not around the flirts of wealth
It requires not the service of your strength
It is the labor of no rewards
Yet, the effort that yields a fruit at the harvest
It is the culture of affection that seems not to rest

The Point of No Return

It is the most valuable point
The point you make or unmake
It is the force after the urge and before the bang of death
Perhaps, victims of such course live to call it the motivator
It is that which yields you not to only admire but to possess
The attraction between the criminal and the crime
The point of no return
The moment between the skin and the ordeal
A journey, sweet or sour; your destiny

Our Paths Are Closer Than You Think

At the dawn of breath, poverty ridiculed the fabric of the day
I have walked the aisle discourteously to the seductively damned flirts
    of the greed's debts
In lack of wealth
The acclamation of recognition, I hide to chide
Although the dice of hope was cast in the mornings of this journey
Although I failed the test of overabundance of nothing
Yet, the harvest of farming, rewards with class
Thus, I walk amid the torture of affluent
I speak to change
Thus, bless the struggle
They seek the riches of nothing in mine yesterday
To guide the strive of your today
Our paths are closer than you think

Osagyefo Dr.

Osagyefo Dr. Kwame Nkrumah
To many you left a country
Some, you left us liberty
Yes, you left us an idea
You left us a cause
Although many disparities evolved in your course
You shall forever remain a legacy
To the black man of the first west
To the race, graced with the best
From the east to the west, you live in the pages of research papers
You are a monument to the era of hope

Light Applause

The wrath of nature has rendered them a taste of the dominant bad
The first begat of civilization
Yet, they dance to the foreign clouds above
The victims of wealthy adventures
Cloaked in the shadows of the sailors exceptionalism
The value of their cause, blackens the light of tradition
The fog of delusional liberties
Enslaves the origin of potentials
My people across the oceans
And when force of fate liberate to illuminate their path
The light applause is offered as a sacrifice
O children of the path of its wrath
The light of generation comes
To expose the stains of the greed
Today; a child of yesterday, will you be the light

Kings and Queens

Where are you from?
I'm from the North
I'm from the South
I'm from the East
I'm from the West
But you are an immigrant
They said to my curiosity
I am a Prince in the native land beyond the seas
I am a Princess from the wild of the oppressed
Yet, you are here for greener pastures
I am a son of the great tribe beyond the horizon
I am a daughter of the land with the beauty I possess
Yet, you seek to serve the oppressive papers of freedom
They all hail from the land of the kings and queens
Where power and war begat princes and princesses
Wake up migrants of hope
You have a dream to the dreams

Good Deeds Bad Name

Tis the weed in the addicted hands of the teenager

Yet, the greens in the addicted hands of the father, mother, and the scientists with permit

Tis the gun in the fatal hands of the criminal

Yet, it is death for order in the lawful hands of the police

Tis the fear of know-how in the grips of your adversary

Yet, the hegemonic stability in your camp

Tis the pill for excitement

Yet a force for sorrow in excessive use

The weed

The gun

The WMD-know how

The ecstasy

Tis the good deeds with a bad name

Two Seasons

Tis either the season of life or the sorrow of death

Lest the overpopulated earth may not bare to breath

Hence the dominion of day and night in the cycle of existence

Where the lords of light and darkness respectively rule to or not to
recompense

Sometimes it is the seasons of the rains or the days of the sun

While the wind foretell the coming of riches to her son

The heat from above will be the rewards of your deeds accordingly

When it is not the season of wealth, then you are wrought with the
bond of poverty

Lest the value of such strive evades with its gravity

Life is graced with the season of marriage and the manifest destiny of
the divorcee

Yet, it occasionally becomes the stolen dreams of the humble
beginners by the union rupture

It comes to the norm of the living

Whether sweet or sour; two seasons

Civil War

They fight amongst themselves
Along the winding terrains of the ideological battle grounds of the minds
Lay the skeletons of conquered ideals
The civil war of
Dreams
Ideas
Values
Aspirations
Forecast
It is the mental warfare
Propagated by the school of thoughts
It is the war of the warriors of academics
Slaughtering the wisdom of the commons
The generational war of liberty
The civil war of rights
Tis the battle of the oppressive past
Yet, the civil war of the repressive future
In the battle ground of today
The civil war of rights and ideas not of blood

African American

African American
It is not only the colour of life in the eye
It is not only the texture of hard labour in the hair
It is not only the look of strength in the physique
Nor the feel of exhaustion in the skin
It is also the bile of slavery endured within the nectar of civilization

African American
It is not only the chain of oppression against the flesh
It is not only the demise of the dreams to the aborigines of the
    repressed generation
It is not only the plight of the fight on board the imperial vessels
Not only the whips of the traders who promised future to the future
    of the kingdoms
It is also the lies of the predators of freedom; the servile flutterers who
    come in the name of kings and queens

African American
It is not the stigma of violence
It is not the loss of culture
It is not the fatherless children
It is the rip of culture that rebrands the original identity

African American
Is the wheel of the industrial vehicle
Is the bullet from the firearms
It is the stolen migrant, who form the spine of a civilization
It is the name of the descendants from the land of riches to the land
    of riches
The children of slavery

The African Woman

Permit me to advertise the beauty of God's Creation

She is the masterpiece of the greatest sculpture

She is a beauty

She carries the weight of the warrior on the entirety of her seducing bosom

On the ensemble of the accuracy of the inviting behind

She is the royal seed of nature

Mother of the future

Mother of warriors

Mother of kings and queens

Mother of a civilization

Mother of mothers

The black woman

She is the light of the dark culture

The black light

The only hope of the left behind

She is the custodian of the original artistry
Molded from the smooth wind of the wild land
Soften with the flexibility of the rivers
Yet, rigid from the ribs of the warriors
She is the African Woman
Sacredly effulgent in beauty
Than the taste of sweetness
Than the feeling of excitement
Than the vision of an eagle
The African Woman
Thus, the wife of dictators
The beauty of wars
The mother of suffrage
She is the queen of anarchy
Bearer of a poet
The softy Princess of the wild Sahara

My Wife

Who do you think bear all this crap of load off of me?
Who do you think burnish the rough edges off myself?
Who do you think cushion my hard nature?
My wife

She is the most beautiful
She is the foundation of my success
The solid thread of love to stitch up my bruised self
She is the beautiful crest of patience in my heart
My wife

She is the rock of unity inside the calamity of my passionate rush
The embodiment of love
A significant pillar of strength to my motivations and achievements
She is the mother
She bears the stress of a stubborn husband
She is my wife

And I flirt as she walks by
And we kissed like teenagers
And it was passionate like a one night stand
Yet, it happens over and over again
Because she is my wife
She said I am her dreams
She said I am the best man ever
She said I am handsome
She sees not my delinquencies
She bid me farewell with kisses each morning as I step into the hustle
    of life;
Reminding me of the heavens that await me at home
She is the home sweet home
And in the shadows of the night,
When the myth of life chase me about in the dreams
In the comfort of my wife's love
I lay my woes

My Mother

My mother
She bare the pain of nine months
She spared me the last for her mouth
Though her path to love swirls about like a labyrinth
Yet, she cared less for my roughness

My mother
When the trials of life hit me hard
When the cycle of success evades me to look so sad
Yet, at the sight of me she smiles to the skies, for the joy of a child
    made her glad

My mother
Though the promise of tomorrow may shine to naught
Though the strife she thrived may reward not
Though the grounds she wished me to gain may seems to trot
Thus, in the pit of frustration she lifts her child not to rot

My mother
Though her age may frail, yet, her love for me remain the same
Though my wrongs may pile up to the lips of foes, yet, she stays to
    care without a pin of shame
And when the fingers of hate will seek to stain me in the lies of greed,
    she stands a wall and finds me no blame

I love you mother
Many a times have I dared your wrath
Yet, in cheers have you loved me to live
Though I fell several times in the path to maturity
Yet, you stood to fend off the pain of nature

If the Future come to Naught

If the future come to naught
Blame not the motivation that bid your intelligence to taught
Let not the whims of frustration leave a spot
But grace your course with sweet memories even as you plot
To recapture your dreams with the weapon of good thoughts
This time your effort will pay with just one shot

I am a Virgin

I am a virgin
I wish to remain the same
Untouched by the foolishness of today's necessity
For I yanked myself out of the beautiful infirmity
That has woven the intricacies of the fabric of a society
Though the forces of peer wishes to subdue the original personality
Yet, I seek not the vengeance of fame
Lest the rewards of tomorrow abound in shame
Thus, I remain untouched by the culture of the popular sin
Though the pleasures of today excites with a grin
I remain a virgin

Broken Mirror

The broken mirror
Revealed the broken face of fate
It is the source of the dilemma
The two dimensional revelation
The present and the future on one reflection
Though the vision is not clear to the aspirations
It has also shattered the prospect of failure
Thus I see not of the element of the past, seeking to steal the future
The way forward lay in the uncertainty of success
The broken mirror of hope
Reveal to life's fate
Less of an image from thy imagination
Thus, obstructive fate, illusioned with the dilemma of the reflection

What is Love

What is love
When it find mine heart appealing not
Though in thy beauty I'm resolve
To the norm of the union's knot'

What is love
When the only crime committed is to be born
With the features undesirable
With the riches of the dreamers fable

What is love
When the only hate in me is to love only you
When the whims of my affection are carried by the dew
Thus, in thy lovely amnesia
I chase a shadow

What is love
When the fate I bear seems down the path Romeos quest for Rosaline
Whilst thy beauty thus, equals Helen
The strife of Troy, I dare not to bear
After all, what is love

The Other Side

The other side
Lays beyond the shores of the unknown
Where the warriors of today have dared not to conquer
The lands of the future inhabited by our ancestors

The other side
Lays the ruin of the other civilization
The town for the second citizens
The people of my people contained by the deterrent of the first

The other side
Lays at the shore of freedom
Yet, enslaved by the castles of the sailors
The traders of manpower, but soldiers in the imperial cause
Yet, we embraced
For along the filth of oppression
Comes the light to a modern revelation

The Rewards of Nature

The rewards of nature
Abounds in its originality
The gifts of life
Evades the worst of times
Thus, they come in the rains or sun
The rewards of nature
Abounds in beauty
Lodges in the camp of them that strive
It may tarry but the seasons of times,
Shall pass when it comes
Yet, they are the products of your effort
The rewards of nature
Carved in the contours of nudity
Amid the serenity of the forest and
The flow of the river lays the strife of hope;
Impeded by the aspirations of life
The rewards of life
The mighty deeds of the things we value less
Remittances from above
The significant cycle
Air to breath
Sun for light
Greens for food
Wild for meat

Freetown 1999

Free off peace
But not free of war
Free off wealth
But not free of health
Free off liberty
But not free of poverty
Free off democracy
But not free of autocracy
Free off super remits
But not free of colonial exploits
Free off the rule of law
But not free of the barbarity I saw
Free off the vast mineral revenues
But not free of hard labour, child labour; they paid their dues
Free off the wild fun
But not free of big brother's gun
Free off its rich tradition
But not free of the new norm; invading transition
Free off the meaning to the purifying blood of its root
But not free of reprisal blood of its future as they shoot
Tis the Freetown of 1999, free off life
But not free of strife

To the souls of the founding fathers,
To souls of the mothers of wars,
To souls of the sons of anarchy,

To the souls of the daughters of torcher of death,

To souls of hateful lynching,

To the souls of the free killers,

To the souls of civil unrest,

To the souls of the ignorant generation,

May you rest in the foundation of our civilization free

Ye victims of proxy wars,

Ye victims of slavery,

Ye victims of colonial commerce,

Ye victims of covet policies,

Ye victims of the supreme benefactor,

Ye victims of greedy politics,

Ye victims of infectious civilization,

May the past remain a horizon,

May we migrate to the free town; the free mind

Freetown

Free mind

Free life

Free death

The values of unity,

Tis a fist of regression,

The norm, the culture

Wonders of Earth

In the mountains of Akuapem
The grace of creation;
The sight of wild as the norm,
The rich tradition of the poor,
Captures the curiosity of admirers
Casting a shadow of wealth,
Of health,
Of influence,
Of beauty,
Of power,
Of an irresistible desire among the lovers of nature
Over the forgotten woes of its dwellers
Tis a land of mysteries;
The birth place of the black prophet, Tutu's shrine;
Anokye, the talisman of peculiar culture
A land of greens, abounds in the wonders of Earth

I Remember

I remember when I was young
When the tales were diluted with the mysteries of the seasons
When the songs talks of a birth
And when the winds brings the chills of HIS fate among men

I remember the holidays
When the clouds descends in the form of cold droplets
When the light of festivities reface the shadows of the night
When the children of faith merry to the life of their inspirations

I remember the season of joy
When the love of the world is evident in the myth of HIS grace
When the tradition of evil is worshiped as the light of a birth
Yet, I merry with all
For HIS dominion rules every breath of life

I remember the peace of the cold season
When the sight of white glows everywhere
When the mysteries of earth's wonders abound in the frozen rains of
    HIS time
Yet the fever of tradition spreads in the likes of humanity

Tunnels of Hope

Amid the tunnels of hope,
The barriers of darkness are the struggle
Death in bits, yet, for a cause they smuggle
Though a cause for good and good
Yet, a course of pain to chasten the survival mood
Sisters in arm, yet, from the loins of one ancestor
Nations of the spine of one history,
Along the corridors of hate; the politics of religion
Zionism or intifada, the tunnels of hope destroys
A tunnel above or a tunnel beneath,
Tis the mouth piece of war,
Where the voices of doom shall rain down a cause
Hence the smiles of success,
At the ends of the tunnels
The tale of two sisters,
The vision for one husband;
The capital

Oh why?

To hell with royalty,
To hell with monarchy,
To hell with the kings and queens of this evil age,
To hell with VIP
Now she is gone
Gone to peace
Gone, away from your accusing fingers,
The fingers of death
The only crime was being a receptionist
Intimidated by the voice of authority
Death by the callers prank
But death by leadership
Lady, rest in peace
Yet the peace of nothing
Oh why?
Why death?
Why not the comfy care of love ones

Beautiful Revelation

I went to bed feeling the weight of years spent for nothing
I wake, reborn to the joy of the promises of something
Yet, for the struggles of tomorrow
I sing it off the memories in sorrow
Though the wrath of achieving naught wrought me to stress
Thus, I ceased to be bound by the norm of benevolence that I serve to
impress
Hence I will place the beauty of the moment amid the reach of mine
aspiration
Lest the tempest greed steals the beautiful revelation
Such is the wandering path of life
When it stabs your naked ambitions as though tis a knife

Look Beyond the Valley

Across the slope of failure
To the hill on the other side
Though the fall may lay steep,
The torture of the valley last enough to bear
Lay down the loads of coded rewards
Lest you share the fate of the martyrs of your quest,
As you approach the rise; the gift of being a warrior
To the slope comes a cliff
The cliff of success,
The cliff of favour
The cliff to your struggles
The see-through reward, paved to sooth your souring feet
At the top lays eternity of possibilities
Thus, look beyond the valley

I am a Beautiful Father

Though I bear the heart of my fathers; Warriors
Though I strive until the bones are rotten
The physique of a man have I; strong one in deeds
The protector of my worlds; my beautiful roses
Yet, I bear the stripes of struggle
The whips of failure
And the vigor of a conqueror;
The temperament of the soul that fuels me to hope
Sad though; the foolishness of a man,
I parted not with
Yet, she smile
On my lap she sat with joy as I stare the hundredth time; the picture
So innocent; her beauty outshines the scattered rage of a father she loves
So I looked the beautiful me; she smiled
I am the shadow; the pillar of her confidence,
I balanced the picture
She tints the roughly dark past
I am a beautiful father

Yet, I Dream

I have grown from the boy to the man
So has the dream; from adventure to survival
Yet, I dream
The nearer I get the farther it appears;
Beyond the horizon of reality,
Amid failure and success I strive
To hold on to the conquered reigns
Yet, I dream
Beyond the lines of ruins
Where I pray for the dream to grow short
Where I pray to wake, living that dream
Yet, I dream
My dream

So Dare Me Failure

I yearn to escape this prison of hope
And acquire the future I own
I yearn to break loose off the tight grips perspicacity
While I let loose the greed to my dreams
I will exhaust any exertion by unfriendly ambitions
So dare me failure
For I stop for no appetizer,
As I run down the prison to my dreams;
Impediment to success
So dare me failure
Dare my ambitions
Dare my motivations

Gloomy Politics

Gloomy politics,
of the enlightened world
they just don't learn
dead in power
Lost to the norms of riches
Gun is death
Gun is money
Freed people of the free world
Why do you live in fear of the enchainment law politics?
While the tradition of death brought to by freedom,
Rules to scare

Love is only a Myth

Love is only a myth,
When it is a feeling of rigid riff
Thus, evokes the epithet; lord of mortals
Creation by the nectar of thrust to her portals
And it squeaks, it shrills,
It cracks to swallow the weights of moans
And when the whims of the myth wrought to naught,
The woes of pleasure turn to groans
For the ensemble of love abound in its mysteries
The myths, the groans and the moans of creation
Thus, in the land of its maturity,
Love dwells not in the lust beyond nakedness
But in the simplicity of its unity
Love is not a myth, love is lovely in reality

A Servant of the Economy

I am burdened by the exuberance of nothing

After every juice of potentials milked by the stress of eight hours

I build empires that harbors the greed of riches

A servant of the economy,

I must run to the time keeper to justify my labor

And when it comes,

It keeps me alive to serve tomorrow

But at the rise of the sun,

My potentials shall be visible beyond the line of surviving

And I will walk in courage to the open arms of rewards

Keep Abreast

You remain the same
A unique fate, short off fame
And perhaps stalled with blame
Thus, I implore there to seek you
Waste not the strength of the self, seeking the ideals of me
Abound in the beauty of the perfect you
The nurtured identity
Keep abreast to the mindset of the great I am
Thus; be not that you will never be

Who is the Rebel?

Who is the rebel?
Is he the soldier for a cause?
Is he among the battalion of enforcers?
Is he the sharp thorns on the course of struggles?
Is he the weapon of the greed or the need?
Is he the by-product of repressive civilization?
Or the talisman of institutional religion and cultural course
Is he the embattled soul of the oppressed?
Is he the charismatic warrior of your nightmares?
Is he the protector or the perpetrator?
Who is the rebel?
He is the soldier
The fighter
Sometimes he is death, for good, for bad

Inaugurate your Voices

Inaugurate hope
Though it hangs on a thin rope
Yes, the rope of fragile consensus
When it seeks to survive, yet, a beauty of an ugly politics
Tis the oath of power
Yes, power to do nothing
Tis hope, but hope on a thin rope
When your franchise is only worth that tradition
Yes, tradition of politics
When the voices you elect, send your dreams down the slope
Yes, the slope of failure
People of the free world
Inaugurate your voice
The voice for the future
The voice with vision

My Girl

(The dilemma of a migrant worker in pigeon language)
An African Public Grammar

My Kiddie want play small saf,
But sake of job,
Man for bed early tonight
My girl,
Make you unna pardon me saf oh

But in the dream saf, yawa oh,
The perfect dream no want come
So so Yankee I just dey think
Hmm, ibe like the mental clock just dey tick
O Papa God adey beg make unna help me small

I figure say I just bed,
But my one eye don open
So say I no bed too much
Hahaha man dey suffer oh, me saf I dey laf ma body

The alarm don dey ring waa
And I just jump,
Like say I be soldier
Ready for war, hehehehe, na
Way kind life be this saf,
Sake of job I just dey go-dey come
Nawaa ooh
Na the summary
Of a migrant
Workers life be this that ooh
Wey kind dream saf
We dey follow follow this

My Girl

(The dilemma of a migrant worker; revised)

Oh forgive me my child
I know you want to play
I know you want that attention
But my girl
I will have to sleep tonight
While my job knocks on my dreams

Oh what world,
So sad that I have to sleep with the clock of labor ticking
Hindering all the sweet dreams; the American dream
Good God be my help

Though I sleep,
My eyes stay open
For the morning comes with labor; our daily bread
Hahaha, to my self

Then the alarm rings,
Indebted to my bills, I jump off the bed like a soldier
Ready for war, heheheh
What a life
I seek the dream of the free world
Thus, the life I live revolves around my job
It is sad
For this is the summary of the migrant worker
But what kind of dream is this
That sends us after currency shadows
that we follow to no avail

Heavens, Such greed of humans!

We have created a haven for the follies of our ambitions,

We seek to dominate beyond the reach of life,

If the threshold of power be unleashed to the greed of homo-sapiens,

If the mysteries beyond the horizon of life be revealed

To the rapacious disposition of mortal beings,

If the eternal dwellings of the soul be known to the wandering
ambitions of humans,

Then, man will seek to conquer the reign of the immortals,

Thus, the celestial source of life

Heavens, such greed of humans!

The greed to outwit the voracious tendencies of humans,

The calamitous greed of man to deny

The omnipresence deposition to the lord of the heavens,

Tis the greed, that permeates the foundations to man's pregnable
aspirations.

Among My Kind

I have toiled and soil my life with their invading strife
Yet, at the dawn of harvest, mine ethnicity betrays, though I strive
O ye toothless pit-vipers of your kind
What happened to whips of labour in the sweet plantation of the canes
Have you now turned to the greed of chickens
Who will hesitate not to devour all your heart giving effort
Yet, wipe it beaks clean as though it has not been fed in ages
What happened to the sweats that washed the grease off the rail-roads
Where the swift strokes of oppression operates my strength to oppose
    my will
Have you now turned to the friend in the shadows
Who will kiss me to my doom
Among the struggles of our rejected rights, I find home
Among the hood of a society, I path out the future alone
Among my kind;
The bound sailors of the forgotten kingdoms

Among my kind;
The servitude builders of the imperial empires
Among my kind;
The daring bearers of the scares of the profiteers' domination
Yes, among my kind;
The dwellers of the ghetto, the slums, the hood and the warring
    kingdoms beyond the oceans
And yes among the people of my people,
I find home,
I find peace,
I am accepted,
Where I toil to soil my life to gain
Where prejudice rules not to the sharing of the harvest

Is This Justice

I ain't done nothing

All I had done was to roam my jobless self on the streets of my
neglected hood

Yet, I spent months under the care of ferocious guards

Spitting instructions to my perplexed face

While the big bosses sit under the fresh air of the poor taxed,

To decide what to do with another brother

Will I become a state property or a problem with coded names?

Is this justice

I refuse to continue the cycle of procreation

Yes, why should I,

While potent brothers and sisters are wasted in the ugly cities of the
beautiful world

Why should another sister be attuned to bordello professions and the
strip mistress?

The only profession awaiting my kind

Is this justice

I yearn to evade the future
When it comes with the impediments of yesterday's legal oppressions
When I am refused the benefits of my potentials
Because the mesh of segregation, is perforated enough to arrest the
    brother's deeds
Because the trade of the ghetto, although inspired by the systemic
    negligence of the bosses rule
Cast a shadow of failure above my human self
Is this justice
Anyway, because I came by the brute of that imperial pirates
Chained against my will
Worked till the juice of life flee me
I share the norm of the horses
Lashed to build the cities of today
Yet we dwell in the slums of its beauty
And die serving a dream that enslaves
Is this justice

If I Don't Say It

If I don't say it, who will address the woes of the people of my people

If I don't say it, who will talk about the cry of the mothers whose children build the cities in a cage

If I don't say it, who will remind them of the fathers whose innocents keep them behind the walls of oppression

If I don't say it; who will tell them, when the bullets from the sky brings the message of death

If I don't say it; who will warn them, when they come to kill by the orders of their faith

If I don't say it; who will say it, when they go to die on the orders of authority and live to them liberty and wealth without the directives of a parent

If I don't say it, who will reveal the plight of their dilemma; as the imported civilization antagonize the culture of their fathers

Ghetto

I live in the great cities of the lights
Amongst the kind; the great minds of my generation that builds
    modern empires
I am under occupation
While the inferior vehicles of civilization
Occupies the inherited lands for cultivation
Thus, along the lousy corridors of riches
The crimes of sophisticated fornication
Spills out the taboos of the night in the alleys of the morning
We, the faceless children of the ghetto
The occupants of the hooded cities amid the capitals of today
We bare the marks of their crime; no identity
As we lay along the streets under the bridges and in the filth of their
    wealth
Ghetto is not a place
But ghetto; the taboo we have become of the creed of their deeds
Ghetto, the forgotten children of their crimes

Weapons of War

The weapons of war are no longer the imposing fear of the artillery
But by the cold hands of the living dead;
The plight of those who wield death
Go to the four corners of the world, the disparities are wide
But the fearful end of its victims; the mortal remains of life align the
    means
Oh Africa, My people, our root;
Why do you send drugged children, our future to kill the fathers, the
    mothers; the bearers of our identity
You kill the fathers to the naught of generation
You kill the mothers to the naught of humanity
While thy brothers and sisters, we live to face the invincible horizon;
Where is the culture?
Where is the tradition?
To our brothers on the east, beyond the center of the sand, the
    birthplace of great religions
I know your plight
Your fear of the invading identities
But let not thy self be the prophecy of doom
To those who defile thy holy customs
Nor should thy demise be the cause to wailing cries of mothers
Of the mothers of thy tribesmen, nor of the mothers from afar,
    beyond the reach of thy doctrines
But let the reality or the myth of thy faith relieve you off thy sorrow

Let it reward or punish the boots that leaves bloody prints of death or
    smiling growth to your future
To the southern people of the northern realm
Great are your numbers
Oh thou Latin cultures of a beautiful world
Why send the mothers to war
The warrior mothers of the rebellion cause
Yield not thy womb to the bloody generals
While you wield death that smokes to the sound, wakening the future
    in thy womb to the horror of today
To the North; the union of the great kingdoms
Your laws to freedom
Are killing the great civilization of the free worshipers
A tale of rights
Doom to the vision of the master builders
Don't become the fading light
The blind path-finders of today's generation
Thus, the weapons of today's war;
The drugged children of our future
The faithful worshipers of great religions
The mothers; the bearers of the future
The laws of great democracy
Thus, the weapons of war are the good things of the gift of Life

The Night Train

When the standards of yesterday are giving way to the stagnant ideals
　　to ponder
When the inherited morals are dying to the dementia morale's modernity
When the norm of reclusive pleasures evolve to devolve the rhythm of
　　natural order
And when the roughness of the alleys of yesterday cast its melancholic
　　spell of equality
Thus, put on the royal grin of the faithful seed
That stood to the whims of civil dexterity
And heed not to the recalcitrant creed
Thus, look to the promise of the night train
Where the remnants of the faithful cause
Will ride to wear the crown fit for royals
Though from whence it comes, we know not
Perhaps in the whims of this dilemma
HE comes on the tracks of the night wind
Amidst the train of celestial warriors
The night train comes with the moon
Thus, fight off the fatigue of sleep; the deceitful decrees of the laws

Dirty Laundry

Keep your dirty laundry in your closet
While I washed out the foreign stain of imperialism
Oh what a free world
Where words like virginity and chastity are vanishing
Yes, vanishing from the lips of humanity
Perhaps hiding in the eloquent storage of the dictionary
Branded, a thing of the past
Tis not free to the chaste of this age
Oh my world
When will you "Sankofa"
Yes, return to your root
Let not the intrusive garment of unchaste virgins be worn
Less, you be riddles by the AUTHOR'S meritorious morals

New Age

It said that we have evolve into a new age

Sadly, the age when the follies of the past serves them a treasure

I must warn, perhaps by the peak of this torture

By the close of my case;

I may be the enemy, the adversary

But, an adversary to that gloomily enlightening age to naught will I prefer,

Hence the wrath from the watchful eyes of the vast sky be eternal

Lest the lines of the Author of life may climax to sour

Perhaps a hiatus to this sweetened music of life will remain to my doom

Should I remain in this age affair

Thus, go; go alone to your new marriage, your new age

Marry your doom

Don't deny me mine inheritance

The heritage of life

When You Have a Child King

When you have a child king
Bloody generals make wars
Whilst the fate of the whimsical adversaries of the young's adventure
Are audaciously driven to naught, at the price of peace's demise
When you have a child king
Young warriors appease their lords, but in death
Yet, the custodians of yesterday are retired to the age of dreamers
For the council of tomorrow belongs to the martyrs of the adventure;
The puppet warriors of a child king
When you have a child king
The banners of solidarity are implicated as foes;
Paving way for the way-laying barons of globalization
And the norm of the common becomes a reward
Yes, a daring reward of the war games; the child's play
Thus, when you have a child king
The politics is thus gloomy,
And fate is only a gift,
The result of nefarious oligarchy,
Yet, an unenlightened civilization

A Revelation of the Living

When you know that your demise is ordained,
Beyond the realm of stars
Beyond the space of nothing
Beyond the reach of life
Thus, your death is no martyrdom
When you know that your success was written,
By the hand of hope
By the author of life
By the suffrage of purity
By the affliction to the TREE
Hence thy feat is no heroism
When you know that the heart was molded by the spirit of authority
The force of charity
The cause to liberate
Thy love to the seeds of life
Is, but your identity
When you know what you know
That you lack the ability to know all you need to know
Not even the clenched fists of the whims off admirations
Sways you to naught
For you are moved by a factor
Thus, by the force of the sight of life
When you exit through the windows of self;
A revelation of the living

Bastard Nobles

Gone are the days,

When peasant birth was sought after,

But by royalties; bastard princes and princesses of great kings

Amid the time when conquering generals will roam eternity

To heed to the butchery bids of their lord masters

Yet, these derelict nobles off bordellos and taverns

A great tool for barons of powerful banners to great heights

Yet, there were days when nobility abdicate its worth

Perhaps days when de-facto lords abrogate inheritance

Thus, there comes a day,

When castles of duplicity will not shield

When the machinery of torture will be crushed beneath the hooves of
    justice

When the credible swords of truth shall strike deep to the heart of
    subterfuge diplomacy

When the nepotistic rule of greedy warriors frails to naught

Because, there comes a day

When the black nights of noble origins;
Bastard nobles flanked by blood,
Will ride to reclaim the inheritance
The forbidden truth of the royal seed
For there comes a time
When you will be apportioned your crown
Notwithstanding the risk of race
Regardless of your idiosyncratic disposition to the veracity of life
Nor berated by the origin of your beginnings;
The bastard nobles

A Lovely Conversation

How is my warrior faring
Not much beautiful
But In my world of dreams,
Feeling your beautiful self,
While fantasying about every potential moment
And all the delicious moments that stands to unfold lovely
Oh really, what could that mental picture be
After all you have that chest of mighty warriors
Hands as strong as several hunters
And the conquering mind as swift as lust before love
Dearest, you asked about the picture of queens
If I should write the pleasure in words,
The ecstasy of the moment will fade to a mere mirage
I will tell you this,
Close your eyes to the filth of this world
As you lay with your ears closed to sweet noise of players of this game
And I will urge you to roam the romancing world of dreams with me
So now my sunshine, do you feel the heat that warms off this frozen
    pull of lust
The dreams I have in my dream
Lay on your back, thus the pressure you feel is the pleasure of this flirtation
Ask me not to yield to you the passion of lovely emotions
Lest I write off the taste of love out of this lovely conversation